# Never Wear Your Wellies in the House

and Other Poems to Make You Laugh

*Collected by Tom Baker*

A royalty on each copy of this book is paid to MENCAP, the National Society for Mentally Handicapped Children and Adults.

# Never Wear Your Wellies in the House

and Other Poems
to Make You Laugh

Collected by Tom Baker

*Illustrated by children from Special Schools.
Organized through MENCAP*

**SPARROW
BOOKS**

A Sparrow Book
Published by Arrow Books Limited
17–21 Conway Street, London W1P 6JD

An imprint of the Hutchinson Publishing Group

London Melbourne Sydney Auckland
Johannesburg and agencies
throughout the world

First published 1981
Arrow edition 1981
Reprinted 1981 and 1982
© In this collection by Tom Baker 1981

Set in Century Schoolbook by
Rowland Phototypesetting Limited
Bury St Edmunds, Suffolk

Made and printed in Great Britain
by The Anchor Press Ltd
Tiptree, Essex

ISBN 0 09 927340 3

# Contents

# Introduction

Tom Baker

'Oh, don't be silly!', 'Don't be so silly!', 'That was just silly!'. Adults say that to children an awful lot and yet they get quite shirty if you say it back to them. Yet what is so silly about doing silly things? Sometimes it's when we are silly we have most fun. Some people might call some of the poems in this book silly but that does not mean they are worthless. Oh no!

Watching T.V., riding your bicycle, playing with your friends is fun. Poetry is fun too . . . and if it's not there's something wrong. We may be misunderstanding poetry because at some time we've read the wrong sort of poetry or read it at the wrong time and been bored by it. Beware! Boredom is a terrible enemy. A demon! It's boredom that suffocates adventure. Silly boredom! Read these poems, drive boredom from your door and have one hundred per cent fun!

The editor and publisher would like to thank all the children in Special Schools who drew the pictures for the book and the teachers who organised the collection of the drawings. In particular, we would like to thank the following children who produced drawings for poems: Sandra from Meadway School for 'The Pig', Veronica from Meadway School for 'Names', Chandra from Kingsbury School for 'The Cat Sat On The Garden Wall', Brian from Harborough School for 'Gruesome', 'The Trials of An Author's Wife', 'Doggerel', 'Upside Down', 'End Of A Girl's First Tooth' and 'Mr Bidery's Spidery Garden', Robert from Ickburgh School for 'Oh, I wish I'd looked After My Teeth', Carole from Ickburgh School for 'Cyril the Centipede', Ruth from Meadway School for 'Mr Kartoffel', Miriam from Ickburgh School for 'The Lion', Richard from Meadway School for the 'Limerick', and 'Never Wear Your Wellies In The House', Julian from Paddock School for 'The Pantomime', Kim from Oaklands School for 'Fingummy . . . .', Surinder from Oaklands School for 'Quack! Said The Billy-Goat', Wayne from Meadway School for 'The Foolish Man', Joan from Paddock School for 'Pennies from Heaven' and Eric from Meadway School for The Walrus.

# What's the Point of Poetry?

*Michael Palin*

'What's the point of poetry?'
Said the starling to the bat –
He'd already asked a weasel
And he dared not ask the cat.
'Ooh, that's too hard for me,'
replied the furry, sightless creature,
'You should fly to Leicester Modern School
And ask the English teacher.'

# The Pig

*Colin West*

The table manners of the pig
Leave much to be desired.
His appetite is always big,
His talk is uninspired.

And if you ask him out to dine,
You'll only ask him once,
Unless you like to see a swine
Who gobbles as he grunts.

# Never Wear Your Wellies in the House

*Tom Baker*

If you want to be as silent as a mouse,
Or jump as high as any little house,
You must nibble lots of cheese,
Say "Hello" to passing fleas
And never wear your wellies in the house.

Stick your neck out just as far as a giraffe,
Be eccentric and you'll make the others laugh
But except when you're alone
When of course you'll feel at home
You should never wear your knickers in the bath.

If you don't want to lie awake in fear and dread,
Or have nightmares all in horrid shades of red,
Nor have crumbs just everywhere,
Twixt your toes and in your hair,
You must never take a currant bun to bed.

If you want to be as silent as a mouse,
Or jump as high as any little house,
You must nibble lots of cheese,
Say "Hello" to passing fleas
And *never* wear your wellies in the house.

# Fingummy...

*Mike Harding*

Fingummy's fat
And Fingummy's small,
And Fingummy lives
With the boots in the hall.

If Fingummy bites,
If Fingummy tears,
If Fingummy chases you
Up the stairs
Shout 'Bumble-Bee Soup
And Bluebottle Jam',
And run up to bed as fast as you can!

'Cos Fingummy lives
Where there's never no light
And Fingummy makes
The dark sounds of the night,
And Fingummy's fat
And Fingummy's small
And Fingummy lives
In the dark, in the hall. . . .

# Names

*Norman Hunter*

Murgatroyd Stephen Montgomery James.
Did you ever hear such a collection of names?
Murgatroyd after his father, you see.
Stephen because of his uncle, that's me.
His mother chose Monty, and she was
    emphatic;
While James, said his aunties, was
    aristocratic.
So he was christened, but isn't it silly?
The only name anyone calls him is Billy.

MURGATROYD
STEPHEN
MONTGOM-
ERY
JAMES

# Pennies from Heaven

*Spike Milligan*

I put 10p in my Piggy Bank
To save for a rainy day.
It rained the *very next morning!*
Three Cheers, Hip Hip Hooray!

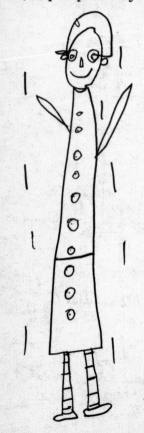

# The Cat Sat on the Garden Wall

*Dyan Sheldon*

The cat sat on the garden wall
and gave the fly a swat.
He meant to hold on very tight . . .
but he didn't. He forgot.

19

# The Cheetah, My Dearest, is Known Not to Cheat

*George Barker*

The cheetah, my dearest, is known not to
   cheat;
the tiger possesses no tie;
the horse-fly, of course, was never a horse;
the lion will not tell a lie.

The turkey, though perky, was never a Turk;
nor the monkey ever a monk;
the mandrel, though like one, was never a
   man,
but some men are like him, when drunk.

The springbok, dear thing, was not born in
   the Spring;
the walrus will not build a wall.
No badger is bad; no adder can add.
There is no truth in these things at all.

# The Pantomime

*Guy Boas*

Regularly at Christmas-time
We're taken to the pantomime;
We think it's childish, but we go
Because Papa enjoys it so.

# The Ants at the Olympics

*Richard Digance*

At last year's Jungle Olympics,
the Ants were completely outclassed.
In fact, from an entry of sixty-two teams,
the Ants came their usual last.

They didn't win one single medal.
Not that that's a surprise.
The reason was not for lack of trying
but more their unfortunate size.

While the cheetahs won most of the sprinting
And the hippos won putting the shot,
the Ants tried sprinting but couldn't,
and tried to put but could not.

It was sad for the Ants 'cause they're sloggers.
They turn out for every event
With their shorts and their bright orange
  tee-shirts,
their athletes are proud they are sent.

They came last at the high jump and hurdles,
which they say they'd have won, but they fell.
They came last in the four hundred metres
and last in the swimming as well.

They came last in the long-distance running,
though they say they might have come first.
And they might if the other sixty-one teams
Hadn't put in a finishing burst.

But each year they turn up regardless.
They're popular in the parade.
The other teams whistle and cheer them,
aware of the journey they've made.

For the Jungle Olympics in August,
they have to set off New Year's Day.
They didn't arrive the year before last.
They set off but went the wrong way.

So long as they try there's a reason.
After all, it's only a sport.
They'll be back next year to bring up the rear,
and that's an encouraging thought.

# Busy Day

*Michael Rosen*

Pop in
pop out
pop over the road
pop out for a walk
pop in for a talk
pop down to the shop
can't stop
got to pop

got to pop?

pop where?
pop what?

well
I've got to
pop round
pop up
pop in to town
pop out and see
pop in for tea
pop down to the shop
can't stop
got to pop

got to pop?

pop where?
pop what?

well
I've got to
pop in
pop out
pop over the road
pop out for a walk
pop in for a talk. . . .

# Upside Down

*Aileen Fisher*

It's funny how beetles
and creatures like that
can walk upside down
as well as walk flat:

They crawl on a ceiling
and climb on a wall
without any practice
or trouble at all,

While I have been trying
for a year (maybe more)
and still I can't stand
with my head on the floor.

# Gruesome

*Roger McGough*

I was sitting in the sitting room
toying with some toys
when from a door marked: 'GRUESOME'
There came a GRUESOME noise.

Cautiously I opened it
and there to my surprise
a little GRUE lay sitting
with tears in its eyes

'Oh little GRUE please tell me
what is it ails thee so?'
'Well I'm so small,' he sobbed,
'GRUESSES don't want to know'

'Exercises are the answer,
Each morning you must DO SOME'
He thanked me, smiled,
and do you know what?
The very next day he . . .

# The Foolish Man

*Christopher Chamberlain*

I knew a man who always wore
A saucepan on his head.
I asked him what he did it for –
'I don't know why,' he said.
'It always makes my ears so sore;
I am a foolish man.
I should have left it off before,
And worn a frying pan.'

# Doggerel

*Elisabeth Beresford*

I'm Henry the dog
With a very long nose.
I barks when they come,
And I barks when they goes.
I'm Henry the dog
With a *beautiful* tail
Which shows my delight
As it wags without fail.
But sometimes I wish
That they'd leave me alone.
I'm Henry, Oh Henry,
Who's guarding his home!

# The Elephant

*Charlotte Hough*

Last Friday an elephant wrote
And asked, 'Can I borrow your boat?'
I liked him a lot
But said he could not.
(I wasn't quite sure if he'd float.)

# Uncle

*Harry Graham*

Uncle, whose inventive brains
Kept evolving aeroplanes,
Fell from an enormous height
On my garden lawn, last night.

Flying is a fatal sport,
Uncle wrecked the tennis court.

# Oh, I Wish I'd Looked After Me Teeth

*Pam Ayres*

Oh, I wish I'd looked after me teeth,
And spotted the perils beneath,
All the toffees I chewed,
And the sweet sticky food,
Oh, I wish I'd looked after me teeth.

I wish I'd been that much more willin'
When I had more tooth there than fillin'
To pass up gobstoppers,
From respect to me choppers
And to buy something else with me shillin'.

When I think of the lollies I licked,
And the liquorice allsorts I picked,
Sherbet dabs, big and little,
All that hard peanut brittle,
My conscience gets horribly pricked.

My Mother, she told me no end,
'If you got a tooth, you got a friend.'
I was young then, and careless,
My toothbrush was hairless,
I never had much time to spend.

Oh I showed them the toothpaste all right,
I flashed it about late at night,
But up-and-down brushin'
And pokin' and fussin'
Didn't seem worth the time – I could bite!

If I'd known I was paving the way,
To cavities, caps and decay,
The murder of fillin's
Injections and drillin's
I'd have thrown all me sherbet away.

So I lay in the old dentist's chair,
And I gaze up his nose in despair,
And his drill it do whine,
In these molars of mine,
'Two amalgum,' he'll say, 'for in there.'

How I laughed at my mother's false teeth,
As they foamed in the waters beneath,
But now comes the reckonin'
It's *me* they are beckonin'
Oh, I wish I'd looked after me teeth.

# Limerick

*Anon*

There was a young lady of Niger
Who smiled as she rode on a Tiger;
   They came back from the ride
   With the lady inside,
And the smile on the face of the Tiger.

# Cyril the Centipede

*Jeremy Lloyd*

Cyril the centipede
Loved playing games,
And his favourite one was football.
And when he played goal
With nine fleas and a mole
Nothing got past him at all.

They played spiders and newts
But his hundred boots
Gave his team very little to do
And the fleas would get bored,
The mole never scored
And the crowd would just stand there and boo.

'Til one awful day the crowd stayed away
And no fans for either side came,
But all said and done
When it's none none none none
It's really not much of a game.
Then Cyril the centipede
Hurt his back leg
The hundre'th one down on the right.
So he used a small stick
And went 99 click,
Now I'm happy to say it's all right,
But he doesn't play goal
Any more – he's retired
Unbeaten, for nobody scored.
Now he just referees
For the spiders and fleas,
And even the mole
Has just scored.

# The Little Dog

*Cannon & Ball*

The little dog had got no home,
He wandered the streets at night.
His little body was oh, so thin –
He looked a terrible sight!

His name was Joey, he still knew that, and
He'd lived in a big, big house.
There he'd been happy, there he'd been loved –
And there he'd gone hunting grouse.

There used to be servants and gardeners,
And Joey never got bossed.
Then Joey went for a walk one day
And got himself tragically lost.

He tried to find his way back home,
But only got farther away;
How he missed his soft, comfy bed
And the games he used to play.

He scavenged for food in dustbins,
And searched for places to lie;
He never wagged his tail any more –
There was always a tear in his eye.

He just kept wandering day and night –
He'd been lost eight months or ten –
Then suddenly someone screamed, 'Joey!' –
For he'd wandered home again!!!

# The Trials of an Author's Wife

*Gavin Ewart*

There once was the wife of a writer
(whose literature didn't excite her)
said: *Wherever one looks*
*there are books, books . . . and BOOKS!*
*He's a bibliophilic old blighter!*

# 'Quack!' Said the Billy-Goat

*Charles Causley*

'Quack!' said the billy-goat,
'Oink!' said the hen.
'Miaow!' said the little chick
Running in the pen.

'Hobble-gobble!' said the dog.
'Cluck!' said the sow.
'Tu-whit tu-whoo!' the donkey said.
'Baa!' said the cow.

'Hee-haw!' the turkey cried.
The duck began to moo.
And all at once the sheep went,
'Cock-a-doodle-doo!'

The owl coughed and cleared his throat
And he began to bleat.
'Bow-wow!' said the cock
Swimming in the leat.

'Cheep-cheep!' said the cat
As she began to fly.
'Farmer's been and laid an egg –
That's the reason why.'

# Bananas

*Carey Blyton*

Bananas,
In pyjamas,
Are coming down the stairs;
Bananas,
In pyjamas,
Are coming down in pairs;
Bananas,
In pyjamas,
Are chasing teddy bears –
'Cos on Tuesdays
They all try to
CATCH THEM UNAWARES.

# The Walrus

*Michael Flanders*

The Walrus lives on icy floes
And unsuspecting Eskimoes.

Don't bring your wife to Arctic Tundra
A Walrus may bob up from undra.

# End of a Girl's First Tooth

*Roy Fuller*

Once she'd a tooth that wiggled;
Now she's a gap that lisps.
For weeks she could only suck lollies;
Now she champs peanuts and crithsps.

# The Lion

*Roald Dahl*

The lion just adores to eat
A lot of red and tender meat,
And if you ask the lion what
Is much the tenderest of the lot,
He will not say a roast of lamb
Or curried beef or devilled ham

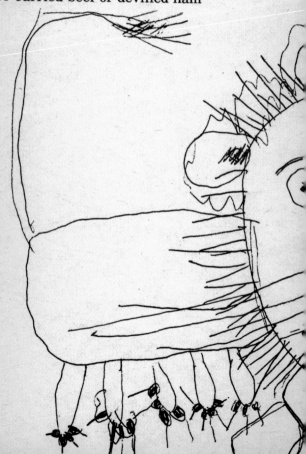

Or crispy pork or corned-beef hash
Or sausages or mutton mash.
Then could it be a big plump hen?
He answers 'No'. What is it, then?
Oh, lion dear, could I not make
You happy with a lovely steak?

Could I entice you from your lair
With rabbit pie or roasted hare?
The lion smiled and shook his head.
He came up very close and said,
'The meat I am about to chew
Is neither steak nor chops. It's you.'

# Christmas Thank You's

*Mick Gowar*

Dear Auntie
Oh, what a nice jumper
I've always adored powder blue
and fancy you thinking of
orange and pink
for the stripes
how clever of you

Dear Uncle
The soap is
terrific
So
useful
and such a kind thought and
how did you guess that
I'd just used the last of
the soap that last Christmas brought

Dear Gran
Many thanks for the hankies
Now I really can't wait for the flu
and the daisies embroidered
in red round the 'M'
for Michael
how
thoughtful of you

Dear Cousin
What socks!
and the same sort you wear
so you must be
the last word in style
and I'm certain you're right that the
luminous green
will make me stand out a mile

Dear Sister
I quite understand your concern
it's a risk sending jam in the post
But I think I've pulled out
all the big bits
of glass
so it won't taste too sharp
spread on toast

Dear Grandad
Don't fret
I'm delighted
So *don't* think your gift will
offend
I'm not at all hurt
that you gave up this year
and just sent me
a fiver
to spend

# Mr Bidery's Spidery Garden

*David McCord*

Poor old Mr Bidery.
His garden's awfully spidery:
Bugs use it as a hidery.

In April it was seedery,
By May a mass of weedery;
And oh, the bugs! How greedery.

White flowers out or buddery,
Potatoes made it spuddery;
And when it rained, what muddery!

June days grow long and shaddery;
Bullfrog forgets his taddery;
The spider legs his laddery.

With cabbages so odoury,
Snapdragons soon explodery,
At twilight all is toadery.

Young corn still far from foddery
No sign of goldenrodery,
Yet feeling low and doddery

Is poor old Mr Bidery,
His garden lush and spidery,
His apples green, not cidery.

Pea-picking *is* so poddery!

# Skinny Winny

*Peter Wesley-Smith*

Skinny Winny
Silly ninny
Took a bath.

Pulled the plug.

Glug glug glug.

Question:
What do you think
Happened to
Skinny Winny?

# Cousin Bert

*Shelagh McGee*

Cousin Bert
Has a very nice shirt
With Christmas trees
And mountains

It's striped and checked
And all bedecked
With polka dots
And fountains.

# Mr Kartoffel

*James Reeves*

Mr Kartoffel's a whimsical man;
He drinks his beer from a watering can,
And for no reason that I can see
He fills his pockets with china tea.
He parts his hair with a knife and fork
And takes his ducks for a Sunday walk.
Says he, 'If my wife and I should choose
To wear our stockings outside our shoes,
Plant tulip bulbs in the baby's pram
And eat tobacco instead of jam
And fill the bath with cauliflowers,
That's nobody's business at all but ours.'
Says Mrs K, 'I may choose to travel
With a sack of grass or a sack of gravel,
Or paint my toes, one black, one white,
Or sit on a bird's nest half the night –
But whatever I do that is rum or rare,
I rather think that it's my affair.

So fill up your pockets with stamps and string,
And let us be ready for anything!'
Says Mr K to his whimsical wife,
'How can we face the storms of life,
Unless we are ready for anything?
So if you've provided the stamps and string,
Let us pump up the saddle and harness the
   horse
And fill him with carrots and custard and
   sauce,
Let us leap on him lightly and give him a
   shove
And it's over the sea and away, my love!'

# Index

The editor and the publisher wish to thank the following for permission to use copyright material in this anthology: Michael Palin for 'What's The Point of Poetry?', Colin West for 'The Pig', Tom Baker for 'Never Wear Your Wellies In The House', Mike Harding for 'Fingummy', Spike Milligan for 'Pennies From Heaven' from *Unspun Socks From A Chicken's Laundry* (Michael Joseph), Norman Hunter for 'Names', George Barker and Faber and Faber Ltd for 'The Cheetah, My Dearest, Is Known Not To Cheat', from *Runes and Rhymes and Tunes and Chimes* (Faber), Richard Digance and Michael Joseph Ltd for 'The Ants At The Olympics' from *Animal Alphabet* (Michael Joseph), Michael Rosen and Andre Deutsch Ltd for 'Busy Day' from 'Mind Your Own Business' (Andre Deutsch), Dyan Sheldon for 'The Cat Sat On The Garden Wall', Roger McGough for 'Gruesome' from 'You Tell Me' (Kestrel), Christopher Chamberlain for 'The Foolish Man', Elisabeth Beresford for 'Doggerel', Charlotte Hough and J. M. Dent for 'The Elephant' from *Verse and Various* (J. M. Dent), Pam Ayres for 'Oh, I Wish I'd Looked After Me Teeth', from *All Pam's Poems* (Hutchinson), Carey Blyton and Faber and Faber Ltd for 'Bananas' from 'Bananas in Pyjamas' (Faber), Guy Boas and A. C. Black for 'The Pantomime' from *Bric A Brac* (A & C Black), Jeremy Lloyd and Chappels Music Ltd for 'Cyril The Centipede' from *Captain Beaky* (Chappel), Gavin Ewart for 'The Trials Of An Author's Wife', Mick Gowar and Collins for 'Christmas Thank You's' from *Swings and Roundabouts* (Collins), Aileen Fisher for 'Upside Down' from *Up The Windy Hill* (Abelard-Schuman), Harry Graham and Edward Arnold for 'Uncle' from *Most Ruthless Rhymes For Heartless Homes* (Edward Arnold), Charles Causley and Macmillan Ltd for ''Quack!' Said The Billy-Goat' from 'Figgie Hobbin' (Macmillan), Roy Fuller and Andre Deutsch Ltd for 'End Of A Girl's First Tooth' from 'Poor Roy', Michael Flanders and the Felix Gluck Press for 'The Walrus', William Heinemann Ltd for 'Mr Kartoffel' from 'The Wandering Moon' (Heinemann), Roald Dahl and Jonathan Cape Ltd for 'The Lion', Peter Wesley and Smith and Angus and Robertson for 'Skinny Winny', Shelagh McGee for 'Cousin Bert' from *Smile Please* (Robson Books), David McGord and George C. Harrap for 'Mr Bidery's Spidery Garden', and Cannon & Ball for 'The Little Dog'.